God Is Everywhere

GOD
Is Everywhere

Inspiring Writings That Reveal His Nearness And Love

Selected by Harold Whaley

Hallmark Crown Editions

The publisher wishes to thank those who have given their kind permission to reprint material included in this book. Every effort has been made to give proper acknowledgments. Any omissions or errors are deeply regretted, and the publisher, upon notification, will be pleased to make necessary corrections in subsequent editions.

ACKNOWLEDGMENTS: "A boy was taken…" by Walter Dudley Cavert from *Remember Now.* Written and copyright renewal 1972 by Walter D. Cavert. Used by permission of Abingdon Press. "God's Music" from *The Mature Heart* by Helen B. Emmons. Copyright 1953 by Pierce & Washabaugh (Abingdon Press). Used by permission of Abingdon Press. "I Have Heard the Song" from *The Gifts of Life and Love* by Ben Zion Bokser. Copyright ©1975 by Ben Zion Bokser. Reprinted by permission of the author. Excerpt from *A Treasury of Albert Schweitzer* by Albert Schweitzer, edited by Thomas Kiernan. Copyright ©1965 by Philosophical Library, Inc. Published by Citadel Press, Inc., and reprinted with their permission. "God's Country" by Louis F. Benson reprinted by permission from *Quotable Poems* compiled by T. C. Clark. "Vestigia" by Bliss Carman from *Bliss Carman's Poems.* Reprinted by permission of Dodd, Mead & Company, Inc., McClelland and Stewart Limited, Toronto, the Canadian Publishers, and by special permission of the Bliss Carman Trust, The University of New Brunswick, Canada. "Letter From Camp" from *We Talk With God* by Lucille E. Hein. Reprinted by permission of Fortress Press. "He Who Owns a Garden" reprinted by permission from *Shamrocks and Prairie Grass* by Katherine Edelman. Copyright 1954 by Katherine Edelman. "Religion in the Curriculum" adapted from *Religious Perplexities* by L. P. Jacks (Harper & Row, 1923). Reprinted by permission of Harper & Row, Publishers, Inc. Second stanza of "So Long as There Are Homes" from *Poems of Inspiration and Courage* by Grace Noll Crowell (1965). Copyright 1936 by Grace Noll Crowell. Reprinted by permission of Harper & Row, Publishers, Inc. Excerpt by E. T. Sullivan from *The Treasure Chest*, edited by Charles L. Wallis. Copyright ©1965 by Charles L. Wallis. Reprinted by permission of Harper & Row, Publishers, Inc. Excerpt from "Beauty" by Glen Bayley from *The Street People.* Copyright 1971 by Judson Press. Reprinted by permission of Judson Press and Hodder and Stoughton Limited. "I Saw God Wash the World" by William L. Stidger reprinted by permission of John W. Hyland, Jr. Four-line excerpt from *Selected Poems and Letters of Emily Dickinson*, edited by Robert N. Linscott. Copyright 1959 by Robert N. Linscott. Reprinted by permission of Elisabeth Linscott, Trustee of the Estate of Robert N. Linscott. "God Our Friend" from *Peace of Mind* by Joshua Loth Liebman. Copyright 1946 by Joshua Loth Liebman. Reprinted by permission of Simon & Schuster, Inc. Excerpt from "I Am There" by James Dillet Freeman reprinted by permission from *Daily Word*, published by Unity School of Christianity.

PHOTOGRAPHS: H. Armstrong-Roberts, pages 22, 39, 46, 49; J. Bilbao (Photo Researchers), page 21; Boy Scouts of America, page 26; Colour Library International, title page; Ed Cooper, pages 6, 11, 30, 45; Jim Cozad, page 18; Peggo Cromer, page 34; Phoebe Dunn, pages 15, 61; Bruce Fizzell, page 61; Peter Fronk, page 33; Kathe Hamilton, page 29; Robert Kolbrener, dust jacket cover, page 57; Ted Laatsh, page 5; Rick Lyons, page 55; Dan Morrill (Vince Kamin), page 43; David Muench, page 16; Lud Munchmeyer, page 37; Willis Peterson, page 8; Bob Segura, page 52; Fred Sieb, page 24; William Weber, page 13; George Whitley (Photo Researchers), page 40; Sam Zarember, page 59.

Can we hear God in a robin's song?
   In the laughter of a child at play?
Can we see Him in the silver symmetry
   of a snowflake or in a sunset?
Perhaps He dwells within our souls
   or in the love we share with friends.
Or, as some claim, He might be heard
      in the thundering chords
         of the organ on Sunday.
            or in the patter of raindrops in April.
But God cannot be found in one place,
   one day, one person.
God is truly in all people, all places,
   all creatures — all creation.
We feel His presence wherever we go,
   in whatever we do…
      because God is everywhere.

from I AM THERE

Do you need Me?
I am there.
You cannot see Me, yet I am the light you see by.
You cannot hear Me, yet I speak through your voice.
You cannot feel Me, yet I am the power at work in your hands.
I am at work, though you do not understand My ways.
I am at work, though you do not recognize My works.
I am not strange visions. I am not mysteries.
Only in absolute stillness, beyond self, can you know
   Me as I am, and then but as a feeling and a faith.
Yet I am there. Yet I hear. Yet I answer.
When you need Me, I am there.
Even if you deny Me, I am there.
Even when you feel most alone, I am there.
Even in your fears, I am there.
Even in your pain, I am there.
I am there when you pray and when you do not pray.
I am in you, and you are in Me . . . .

James Dillet Freeman

"How do you know," a Bedouin asked,
    "that there is a God?"
    "In the same way," he replied,
    "that I know, on looking at the sand,
    when a man or beast
    has crossed the desert —
    by His footprints
    in the world around me."

Henry Parry Liddon

6

WHEAT FIELD

There never was a sight more lovely
Than a field of growing wheat.
Its beauty never ceases, never wanes;
My soul absorbs its peace.
A wheat field is the place
Where I most nearly see the wind;
Very low the whole field bows,
Then rises proud and tall again.
A wheat field is a sea of quiet waves
Flowing freely, though rooted to the earth.
And then when harvesttime has come
And man walks forth to claim its promised good,
He cuts the grain and gathers it in sheaves,
He does but change its beauty —
Here now stand rows of warm-brown altars!
The field becomes a holy place
At sight of which my heart cries out
To thank the Giver of all good.

Myrtle Olga Moll

LOVE ALL GOD'S CREATION

Love all God's creation, both the whole and every
grain of sand. Love every leaf, every ray of light.
Love the animals, love the plants, love each
separate thing. If you love each thing you will perceive
the mystery of God in all; and when once you perceive
this, you will from that time on grow every day
to a fuller understanding of it until you come at last
to love the whole world with a love that will then
be all-embracing and universal.

Feodor Dostoevski

*G*od is an utterable sigh, planted
in the depths of the soul.

Jean Paul Richter

9

Why should I wish to see God better than this day?
I see something of God each hour of the twenty-four,
    and each moment then,
In the faces of men and women I see God, and in my
    own face in the glass,
I find letters dropped in the street, and every one
    is signed by God's name,
And I leave them where they are, for I know that
    wheresoe'er I go
Others will punctually come forever and forever.

Walt Whitman

I sought to hear the voice of God
        And climbed the topmost steeple,
    But God declared: "Go down again —
        I dwell among the people."

John Henry Newman

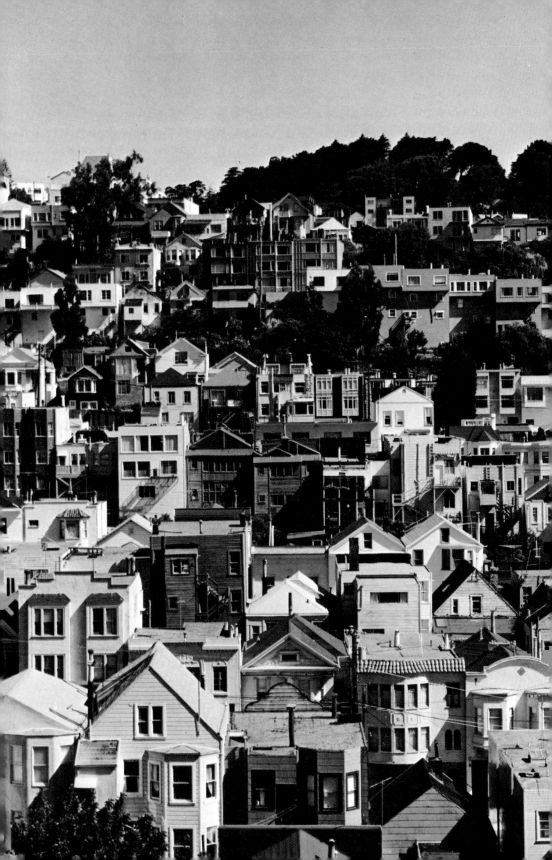

VESTIGIA

I took a day to search for God,
And found Him not. But as I trod
By rocky ledge, through woods untamed,
I saw His footprint in the sod.

Then suddenly, all unaware,
Far off in the deep shadows, where
A solitary hermit thrush
Sang through the holy twilight hush —
I heard His voice upon the air.

And even as I marvelled how
God gives us Heaven here and now,
In a stir of wind that hardly shook
The poplar leaves beside the brook —
His hand was light upon my brow.

At last with evening as I turned
Homeward, and thought what I had learned
And all that there was still to probe —
I caught the glory of His robe
Where the last fires of sunset burned.

Back to the world with quickening start
I looked and longed for any part
In making saving Beauty be.
And from that kindling ecstasy
I knew God dwelt within my heart.

Bliss Carman

A CHILD'S THOUGHT OF GOD

They say that God lives very high!
But if you look above the pines
You cannot see our God. And why?

And if you dig down in the mines
You never see Him in the gold,
Though from Him all that's glory shines.

God is so good, He wears a fold
Of heaven and earth across His face —
Like secrets kept, for love, untold.

But still I feel that His embrace
Slides down by thrills, through all things made,
Through sight and sound of every place:

As if my tender mother laid
On my shut lids, her kisses' pressure,
Half waking me at night; and said,
"Who kissed you through the dark, dear guesser?"

Elizabeth Barrett Browning

The finger of God touches your life
when you make a friend.

Mary Dawson Hughes

from BEAUTY

The waves roll and smash themselves into nothing
   as they crawl upon the beach.
You stand there and look out.
The sea and sky seem to fuse into one
   at the farthest point; wherever that may be.
The bright sun reflecting across the glassy water
   splitting the blue into two converging masses.
The loud but pleasing thunder as the waves collide
   among the smooth time-worn rodes.
The foam bubbling over like a giant sea monster
   emerging from beneath the surface
   and spreading out to swish between your toes.
And think of the one who created all this.
How magnificent He must be; beyond our comprehension.

Glen Bayley

*T*he sea is God's thoughts spread out.

Charles Morgan

from GOD IS: I AM

God is light: the light of brilliant noontide and
the wonder of the stars in a clear night sky, the gleam
of the flickering candle and the flash of the lightning,
the sole source of color, the light of Truth, the light
of wisdom and understanding, and physical, mental, and
spiritual illumination of all sorts and times and
places. Light is God.
    God is love: the affection of friend for friend, the
tenderness of mother for child, the adoration of the
lover for his love, the faithful devotion of a dog to
his master, the deep and abiding love of the long and
happily married husband and wife. These are all but
faint suggestions of the power and the limitlessness of
the love of God for each human spirit. Love is God.

Gordon Parker

19

THE CITY

Outside my window, there are no mountain streams or
fields of flowers. In these places, I know God dwells
in all His majesty. But I am of the city. Beneath my
window, buses wheeze to a halt and trucks rumble by,
delivering their goods. During the night, instead of
the music of crickets, I hear the clang and clatter of
steel against steel as wheels of a freight train roar
over tracks two blocks away. The morning song of birds
mingles with the din of people going to work, and even
the sunrise is blocked from view by concrete giants,
twenty stories high. The sounds I hear would be harsh
to some. And asphalt and neon might appear barren.
But just as the seed finds a home in God's soil, so my
home is in the city. I have grown up thrilling to its
heartbeat, ever confident that its rhythm, too,
is the work of God.

Tina Hacker

*G*od cannot be found on a microscopic slide,
but in the hearts of men.

Edgar Magnin

20

APRIL AFTERNOON

The hills of spring proclaim
God alive and near —
And I lift my heart
In paeans of praise to Him
For returning orioles
And nodding daffodils!

God speaks —
The earth resounds
With the cadence of freshets
And wind rejoicing in new green trees.
It is evident there is only Life.

To be vibrantly awake
To this renascent beauty,
Knowing there are forever new beginnings,
Is ample cause for celebrating
The overwhelming joy of being
On this astounding April afternoon!

Harold Whaley

SIGNATURE

Everywhere I find the signature, the autograph
of God, and he will never deny his own handwriting.
God hath set his tabernacle in the dewdrop as surely
as in the sun. No man can any more create the smallest
flower than he could create the greatest world.

Joseph Parker

A church is God between four walls.

Victor Hugo

RELIGION IN THE CURRICULUM

We teach it in arithmetic by accuracy.
We teach it in language by learning to say what
    we mean — "yea, yea" or "nay, nay."
We teach it in history by humanity.
We teach it in geography by breadth of mind.
We teach it in handicraft by thoroughness.
We teach it in astronomy by reverence.
We teach it by good manners to one another
    and by truthfulness in all things.

L. P. Jacks

LETTER FROM CAMP

Dear Mom and Dad
and Bill and Glad:

Caught a fish.
Camp's a wow!
Sleeping out is grand.

Swimming's fun.
Hiking's fine.
Food is full of sand.

Fire at night.
Moon is bright.
I'm all right.
God's at hand.

Have to run.
Your son . . . Brad.

MIRACLE

We muse on miracles who look
    But lightly on a rose!
Who gives it fragrance or the glint
    Of glory that it shows?

Who holds it here between the sky
    And earth's rain-softened sod?
The miracle of one pale rose
    Is proof enough of God!

Edith Daley

I do not believe in God, for that implies
an effort of the will —
I see God everywhere!

Jean Favre

I HAVE HEARD THE SONG

I have not seen the robin, but I know he is there because
I heard him singing through my window from the treetop
outside.

I have not seen God. But I have looked at my child's
eyes, and have been overwhelmed by the miracle of
unfolding life.

I have watched the trees bedeck themselves with new
garbs of green in the spring, and have been stirred by
the miracle of continual rebirth.

I have looked at the stars, and have been overcome by
the miracle of the grandeur and majesty of the universe.

I know that God exists, because I have heard the song
of His presence from all the treetops of creation.

Ben Zion Bokser

*S*ome people talk about finding God —
as if He could get lost.

Author Unknown

GOD'S COUNTRY

Who shares his life's pure pleasures,
And walks the honest road,
Who trades with heaping measures,
And lifts his brother's load,
Who turns the wrong down bluntly,
And lends the right a hand,
He dwells in God's own country,
He tills the Holy Land.

Louis F. Benson

*I*t is only by forgetting yourself
that you draw near to God.

Henry David Thoreau

There is a God within us, and we glow
when He stirs us.

Ovid

THE JEWISH MOTHER

Jewish custom bids the Jewish mother, after her
preparations for the Sabbath have been completed on
Friday evening, kindle the Sabbath lamp. That is
symbolic of the Jewish woman's influence on her own home,
and through it upon larger circles. She is the inspirer
of a pure family life whose hallowing influences are
incalculable; she is the center of all spiritual endeavors,
the confidante and fosterer of every undertaking. To
her the Talmudic sentence applies: "It is woman alone
through whom God's blessings are vouchsafed to a house."

Henrietta Szold

from SO LONG AS THERE ARE HOMES

So long as there are homes where fires burn
And there is bread;
So long as there are homes where lamps are lit
And prayers are said;
Although people falter through the dark —
And nations grope —
With God himself back of these little homes —
We have sure hope.

Grace Noll Crowell

But if the great sun move not of himself, but is as
an errand-boy in heaven; nor one single star can revolve,
but by some invisible power; how then can this one
small heart beat; this one small brain think thoughts;
unless God does that beating, does that thinking,
does that living, and not I?

Herman Melville

I sought my soul,
      But my soul I could not see.
I sought my God,
      But my God eluded me.
I sought my brother,
      And I found all three.

William Blake

GOD OUR FRIEND

In this vast universe
There is but one supreme truth —
That God is our friend!
By that truth meaning is given
To the remote stars, the numberless centuries,
The long and heroic struggle of mankind . . .
O my Soul, dare to trust this truth!
Dare to rest in God's kindly arms,
Dare to look confidently into His face,
Then launch thyself into life unafraid!
Knowing thou art within thy Father's house,
That thou art surrounded by His love,
Thou wilt become master of fear,
Lord of life, conqueror even of death!

Joshua Loth Liebman

I SAW GOD WASH THE WORLD

I saw God wash the world last night
   With his sweet showers on high,
And then, when morning came, I saw
   Him hang it out to dry.

He washed each tiny blade of grass
   And every trembling tree;
He flung his showers against the hill,
   And swept the billowing sea.

The white rose is a cleaner white,
   The red rose is more red,
Since God washed every fragrant face
   And put them all to bed.

There's not a bird, there's not a bee
   That wings along the way
But is a cleaner bird and bee
   Than it was yesterday.

I saw God wash the world last night.
   Ah, would he had washed me
As clean of all my dust and dirt
   As that old white birch tree.

William L. Stidger

WATCHING CLOUDS

Whenever I see clouds forming pictures in the sky,
I wonder if God is experimenting--seeing what
new works He would like to invent and trying out
different shapes and sizes. I wonder if this is how
our world began. Perhaps God practised first with clouds,
perfecting and polishing His ideas until He was ready
to begin the Creation.

Blanche Harris

I can see how it might be possible
for a man to look down upon the earth
and be an atheist, but I cannot conceive
how he could look up into the heavens
and say there is no God.

Abraham Lincoln

GOD'S MUSIC

God's music is in our ears everywhere in his beautiful
world. We hear it in hurrying streams, sighing winds,
singing birds, falling waters, and lapping waves. But
deeper still we hear it in our hearts when we stop to
listen. It comes in martial strains calling us to work
and to the service of our fellow men. It comes in
softer melody calling us to rest and contemplation.
Again it comes in triumphant strains from another world
when the gates open and loved ones enter in . . . .

There is music in a mother's love, a child's trust,
a happy home, a brave man's battle for a better world,
an unselfish act, a kindly deed. There is "a mighty
music echoing, far and near."

Helen B. Emmons

*G*od is at the organ;
I can hear
A mighty music echoing,
Far and near.

Egbert Sandford

A boy was taken by his father on a camping trip in the Adirondacks. They hired a guide, left the beaten trails, and spent a week in the heart of the woods. The boy was greatly impressed by the ability of the guide to see all sorts of things, invisible to the ordinary eye. One day, after the guide had been pointing out some of the hidden secrets of nature, the lad asked with an awed voice, "Mister, can you see God?"

The old man replied, "My boy, it's getting so I can hardly see anything else when I'm out in the woods."

Walter Dudley Cavert

When I heard
the church bells ring
I thought I heard
the voice of God.

Albert Schweitzer

47

HE WHO OWNS A GARDEN

He who owns a garden,
   However small it be,
Whose hands have planted in it
   Flower or bush or tree;
He who watches patiently
   The growth from nurtured sod,
Who thrills at newly opened bloom
   Is very close to God.

Katherine Edelman

Nature is the art of God.

Dante

When you have shut your doors,
        and darkened your room,
remember never to say that you are alone;
for God is within and your genius is within,
and what need have they of light to see
what you are doing?

Epictetus

THE OPEN DOOR

You, my son,
Have shown me God.
Your kiss upon my cheek
Has made me feel the gentle touch
Of Him who leads us on.
The memory of your smile, when young,
Reveals His face,
As mellowing years come on apace.
And when you went before,
You left the gates of heaven ajar
That I might glimpse,
Approaching from afar,
The glories of His grace.
Hold, son, my hand,
Guide me along the path,
That, coming,
I may stumble not,
Nor roam,
Nor fail to show the way
Which leads us home.

Grace Coolidge

CLOSE TO GOD

Here on these hills no sense of loneliness
Touches my soul. When the long days are fine,
And I can see for miles on miles the line
Of far-off mountains where their summits press
Against the arching azure of the skies.
Or when rain blots all objects out from me
But the dim outline of the nearest tree,
And little sounds so strangely magnifies,
I am content. Peace on my soul descends.
No unfilled longings rise in me to choke
My will. I smell the fragrance of damp sod
Whose pungency with forest odors blends;
And from my shoulders, like an outworn cloak,
My troubles fall, so close to me seems God.

P. L. Montgomery

GOD'S MOST PRECIOUS GIFT

God's gift to us?
What could it be?
The sky, the ocean,
the symmetry of a rose in bloom?
No, not these...
The smile upon a child's face,
a happy home,
a corner in the garden
where we can pause
and reflect
on life's designs?
No, not these...
God's gift to us
is a mighty task--
to finish His world.
We have songs yet to sing,
cities to build,
highways to construct.
We have scientific facts to discover,
the atom to tame,
and the secrets of nature
to explore.
God's most precious gift to us
is opportunity.
In finishing His world--
we come close to Him.

George Webster Douglas

ALL GOODNESS

God is a light
   that is never darkened,
An unwearied life
   that cannot die,
A fountain always flowing,
   a garden of life,
A seminary of wisdom,
   a radical beginning
     of all goodness.

Francis Quarles

The world is charged with the grandeur of God.
It will flame out,
   like shining from shook foil....

Gerard Manley Hopkins

THE GREATEST FORCE

When God wants a great work done in the world or a great
wrong righted, he goes about it in a very unusual way.
He doesn't stir up his earthquakes or send forth
his thunderbolts. Instead, he has a helpless baby born,
perhaps in a simple home and of some obscure mother.
And then God puts the idea into the mother's heart,
and she puts it into the baby's mind. And then God waits.
The greatest forces in the world are not the
earthquakes and the thunderbolts. The greatest forces
in the world are babies.

E. T. Sullivan

Who has not found the heaven below
Will fail of it above.
God's residence is next to mine —
His furniture is love.

Emily Dickinson

GOD IS EVERYWHERE

In a song on the air
The rose in bloom
A prayer in a quiet room.

In the rain and thunder
In the sunshine from the sky
He is in the sea,
In the heart of You and Me.

In the touch of Your hand
In a smile
In the face of each child.

He is in each sharing deed
And gentle word.
He is in the darkest night
And in the echo on a windy hill.

Katherine Ann Dunleavey

Set in Goudy Old Style.
Script on dust jacket and title page
hand-lettered by Norval Arbogast.
Printed on Hallmark Crown Royale Book paper.
Designed by William Hunt.